DRIVING A
SMART
BARGAIN

How to Get the Best Possible Price,

Buying or Selling

J. C. ROBERTON

PAGE PUBLISHING
Meadville, PA

U.S. Federal Copyright
Registration # TX 9-449-603

First originally published by Page Publishing 2019

Cartoon Illustrations by Peter L. Brown
Copyright © 2019

ISBN 978-1-68456-244-2 (pbk)
ISBN 978-1-68456-245-9 (digital)

Printed in the United States of America

Contents

This book is dedicated to those who seek
not just to read, but to learn.

A Note from the Author

My Sources

This book distills the bargaining principles I've learned over a career navigating transactions both as a corporate lawyer and a real-estate principal, as well as several years managing a major medical project in the Middle East.

I didn't learn any of this from classroom theory or other formal studies. I learned it all myself, the hard way, from my own personal experiences in the school of hard knocks. I focused on these pointers one nugget at a time, and I kept notes as I went along. Eventually I crystallized them and put them into writing, to use as a reference to guide myself in my own personal endeavors. My wonderful wife suggested that I write this all up as a book to share with others who may have an interest in the subject. So here it is.

My Writing Style

I choose my language carefully, and I use it sparingly. As a consequence, this book doesn't easily lend itself to being "skimmed." It is most profitably read, savored, and digested, one morsel at a time.

How To Use This Book

This is a reference book, something like an encyclopedia. It offers a variety of independent comments at different places within the text. Readers can benefit by hopping from one spot to another, depending on their needs at the moment.

For this reason, most readers find the printed paper version of this book more useful than the e-book version.

PART I

Introduction

All men have eyes, but few have the gift of penetration.

—Niccolo Machiavelli

What This Book Is All About

This book addresses the very core of capitalism:

- The Seller owns (or can make) the only Commodity in existence and wants to sell it at the highest price possible.

- The Buyer is the only person in existence who has any use for the Commodity and wants to buy it at the lowest price possible.

- How do they arrive at a mutually agreeable price?

And most important for you, the reader, What can you learn from this process to get the best possible deal for yourself?

THE PLAYERS

My Audience

This book is written for the Executives and the Entrepreneurs, the key self-starters who make the wheels go around *for real* across the length and breadth of a free-market economy. These practitioners create the backbone for broad-based economic prosperity as they slug it out every day in the trenches and the arenas of competitive markets.

But this book is also written for the ordinary consumer, the man or woman who, after finalizing a transaction, walks away with the nagging feeling that they might possibly have gained a higher selling price (or a lower purchasing price), if only they knew how to play the game.

This book is written to show you how to play the game.

Why Read This Book?

How much do you have at stake?

The more you have at stake in a given transaction, the more important it is for you to learn and follow the guidelines articulated in this book.

To the Seriously Ambitious Reader

Just casually thumbing through these pages won't automatically make you a good bargainer.

But this book can be a purposeful guideline for those among you with a "fire in the belly," those who are willing to devote serious effort to mastering the principles and techniques articulated here.

This takes work. That means time, dedication, and practice. It may summon you to reexamine some of the teachings you soaked up so conscientiously in your long-ago classrooms. But this approach can add powerful new dimensions to your arsenal of competitive business practices.

Approach this adventure eagerly, actively, and aggressively. Don't be bashful about it; assert yourself. Your opponent expects you to play to win and respects you when you do so.

This may seem awkward at first, but keep at it and you'll find doors that had been closed to you are starting to open.

As you get better at bargaining, you'll become a far more effective executive, a far more effective entrepreneur.

My Scope

This is *not* a compendium of ethics prescribing how anyone *should* conduct themselves. It's a book of objective observations that describes how the game has, *in reality*, been played, ever since our ancestors first began walking upright on two legs. And that's how it's still being played today.

The principles of bargaining are universal, and they are timeless.

My Mission

Despite their timeless universality, many of the principles articulated in this book are not widely known. Why? Because experienced bargainers like it that way. It helps them perpetuate their advantage over the inexperienced.

This book can be particularly helpful for the "little guy," the inexperienced bargainer who might otherwise be taken to the cleaners by more experienced bargainers. The lessons contained here can help level the playing field.

Bargaining can be taught. Bargaining can be learned. Bargainers are made, not born.

THE WINDOW

Your Window of Opportunity

This book addresses what happens within a defined window of time. That window begins when two parties start contemplating the possibility of a mutually beneficial trade, and it ends when the parties clinch the deal (either by consummating the trade or by entering into an enforceable agreement on the terms of trade).

Within this window, bargaining is a unique ball game, governed by its own conventions, its own expectations, its own customs and etiquette. Patterns of behavior that may not be acceptable elsewhere will be expected, and accepted, as key tactics in the game of bargaining.

This book does not address anything that takes place outside of the bargaining window. In particular, this essay does not deal with the performance or implementation of a deal once it has been agreed to.

THE VERY FIRST BARGAINERS

"Bargaining" versus "Negotiating"

These two terms are sometimes used interchangeably to refer to any process of communication in which two or more parties are attempting to reach an agreement on a matter of mutual interest. But I differentiate those two terms in this book.

"Bargaining" (as I use it here) refers to the process of communication that's directed solely at one factor, namely the price at which a given Commodity is bought and sold. In this sense, "bargaining" is synonymous in everyday usage with "haggling" and "dickering."

"Negotiating," on the other hand, can encompass communications dealing with a wide variety of topics or subtopics, all of which must be agreed to before any final deal is concluded. Examples of negotiated transactions are (a) labor-management union contracts, (b) diplomats hammering out an international treaty, (c) acquisition deals in which one company buys an ongoing business from another, (d) police dealing with a hostage standoff, (e) legislators shepherding a bill through the parliamentary processes, and (f) any purchase of residential or commercial real estate.

This book deals exclusively with "bargaining" over the sole subject of price.

Some writers (and there are many) who deal with the general subject of "negotiating" are far too quick to gloss over the question of price. They treat "haggling" or "dickering" as a detail unworthy of serious attention. But in any "negotiated" commercial deal, price is almost always, by far, the most important single item on the agenda.

Proper bargaining over price requires attention to a wide variety of crucially significant matters. Those matters constitute the substance of this book.

A Special Note on Deception

Many competitive endeavors (such as football, baseball, and poker) entail attempts to fool one's opponent, *but always within the rules*. This is not only considered necessary to the game, it's accepted by all concerned as a legitimate part of the contest.

Bargaining is no different. *Within your window of opportunity*, "deception" is a crucial part of the game. Therefore, I've incorporated "Deception" into this book as one of the four key principles of bargaining.

In bargaining, as in most sporting events, the contests are best when the opponents are evenly matched.

Your opponent will be doing everything he can to try to fool you. You can count on that. He will expect you to do the same. Your goal is to get the best possible price for yourself. You fight fire with fire. *Caveat emptor* remains the name of the game.

PART II

The Basics

What Is Bargaining?

The Concept

Millions of commodities (sometimes tangible physical products, sometimes services) are bought and sold everywhere, in countless transactions, on countless markets, every day.

These transactions take two fundamentally different formats:

- *Set Price.* This is established by the seller with no leeway for the Buyer to talk the Seller into taking anything different. An example is buying a can of beans at your local supermarket. You can't debate the price with the clerk at the checkout counter. You either pay the listed price, or you don't get the product. Set-price transactions are most common for those less expensive, ordinary "small-ticket" items that we buy every day.

- *Bargained Price.* This is a unique price arrived at by agreement between the Buyer and the Seller after a give-and-take process of "bargaining" (sometimes referred to, as "dickering" or "haggling"). Bargaining sets the price for some smaller transactions, such as yard sales, flea markets, and antique sales. But bargaining sets the price for *virtually all seriously expensive items*, such as a parcel of real estate or an ongoing business operation.

This book describes the process of bargaining.

The ability to bargain is a necessary condition for serious financial success in a free market economy. The big-ticket items are priced by bargaining. If you don't bargain, you don't play in the Big Leagues.

The Money

MAP (of the Seller): This is the Seller's Minimum Acceptable Price, below which the Seller cannot make money creating and selling this Commodity

MAP (of the Buyer): This is the Buyer's Maximum Acceptable Price, above which the Buyer cannot make money buying and using this Commodity

DEAL ZONE: This is the price range between the Seller's MAP and the Buyer's MAP

Any transaction anywhere within the Deal Zone (DZ) will make some money for the Buyer and some money for the Seller.

The question is, Where, within the DZ, does the transaction take place? Who gets how much of this money?

THE DEAL ZONE

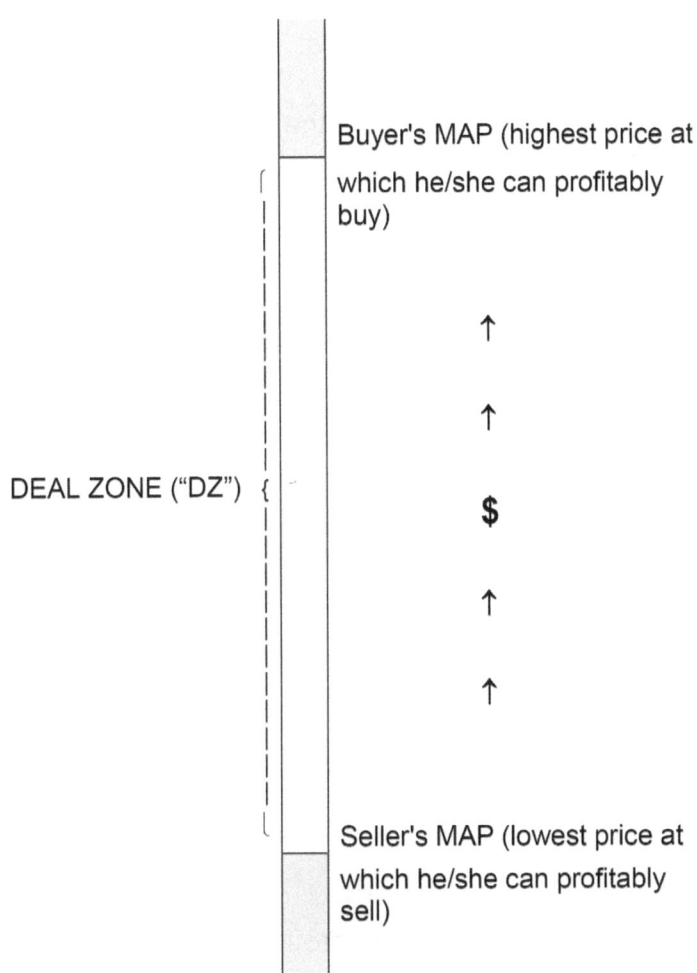

Buyer's MAP (highest price at which he/she can profitably buy)

DEAL ZONE ("DZ")

Seller's MAP (lowest price at which he/she can profitably sell)

The Procedure

Bargaining procedure consists of offers and counteroffers.

- Player A makes an offer.

- Player B either accepts the offer or (taking a risk) rejects and counteroffers.

- Player A either accepts the counteroffer or (taking a risk) rejects and counteroffers.

This continues, until either

- one player accepts, hence they reach a deal, or

- either player terminates the bargaining for any reason.

The *amount of time* that it can take to reach a deal (or terminate the bargaining) varies from seconds to years.

The *number of rejections and counteroffers* that it can take to reach a deal varies from one to thousands.

But the underlying principles remain the same.

The Pressures

At every step of offer or counteroffer, the offeree (who has received the offer) is looking at

- a more generous offer than the preceding one had been and

- a greater likelihood that the offeror (who has extended the offer) will walk away from the bargaining table if Player A rejects and counteroffers.

With every step, acceptance gets more and more attractive; rejection and counteroffer gets less and less attractive.

What Is Risk?

When a player rejects an opponent's offer and makes a counteroffer, that opponent can then either

- accept the counteroffer, or

- reject the counteroffer and make a responsive counteroffer or

- walk away from the bargaining to pursue other options elsewhere.

A player's "risk" in rejecting and counteroffering is measured by how badly that player will be damaged if the opponent chooses the third option (i.e., decides to walk away and leave that first player high and dry without any deal at all).

To the extent a player can absorb such a downside result without being badly damaged, he/she is better able to take a risk. To the extent a player would be badly damaged by such a downside result, he/she is less able to take a risk.

Your Starting Assumptions

Your goal is to get the best possible price for yourself. To achieve your goal it's imperative that you remain focused on those factors, and those dynamics, that will be most powerful in getting you to your goal.

Bargaining isn't a walk in the park. In brutal reality, it can be dusty and dirty, messy and muddy. It's a rough-&-tumble contest, not always pretty. Powerful emotions and distractions of all sorts, some noble and some not so noble, will inevitably get caught up in this intense arena.

This book abstracts, and brings out front & center, those factors that ultimately make the difference between success and failure in the great game of bargaining.

In order to bring these critical factors into the clearest possible focus, I have deliberately cut out of the picture many of the "red herrings" or other irrelevant distractions that often clutter up the scene in the bargaining arena. My technique for doing this is to articulate "Starting Assumptions". This approach distills the bargaining process into its purest theoretical form for purposes of analysis. It helps you view the forest without being distracted by the trees.

Then, when you descend back into the arena of the real world, you'll have the big advantage of being able to stay focused on what's important, and why.

The following are some of the key Starting Assumptions we work with in this book.

- Each player competes all-out for the sole purpose of concluding a final deal on the subject-matter at hand at the best possible price he can get. Neither player is pursuing any ulterior motive. There are no back-door kickbacks or sweet-heart deals involved here.

- A player who makes an offer is ready, willing and able to conclude a deal at that price if the other player accepts. Therefore a player can clinch a deal at any time by accepting his opponent's offer.

- A player who makes an offer sets it at a price where he believes his opponent can make money by accepting. No rational player ever deliberately makes an offer outside the Deal Zone, i.e., higher than Buyer's MAP or lower than Seller's MAP.

- Either player is free to terminate the bargaining process for any reason and walk away from the discussions, at any time before any final deal is concluded.

- Each player works closely with a carefully-chosen lawyer at every step of the game, hence avoids doing anything that could lead to civil or criminal penalties.

A Special Word for the Novice

One of the first things an observer can see is that the opposing players in this game are not always evenly matched.

- Some people engage in bargaining frequently, hence are familiar with many (or at least some) of the tricks and techniques that I cover in this book.

- Others dabble in this type of endeavor only occasionally.

- And far too many naive souls are "little guys," inexperienced bargainers who wander into the game without a clue how to play it.

This book should be especially helpful for those "little guys," novices who may have spent their lives assuming that everything they want to buy or sell can be bought or sold only at the "set price" quoted by their opponents and who have traditionally had little or no inkling that they can get a better financial deal for themselves *if they know how to play the game.*

The typical "little guy" will almost certainly come up against an experienced bargainer now and then. *If that novice doesn't know how to play the game, that experienced bargainer can take him to the cleaners.*

In bargaining, as in most sporting events, the contests work best when the opponents are evenly matched.

This book should help level the playing field, for all concerned.

Bargaining can be taught. Bargaining can be learned.

Bargainers are made, not born.

EVENLY MATCHED?

Win-Win or Win-Lose?

Any transaction anywhere within the Deal Zone (i.e., above the Seller's MAP and below the Buyer's MAP) will make some money for the Buyer and some money for the Seller.

This leads some happy-face commentators to gush that *any* deal within the DZ is therefore a marvelously wonderful "win-win" result, since both players have profited from the trade. The implication is that everybody goes home delighted with what they've gained, and everybody lives happily ever after.

> *Warning!*
> *Don't believe this for a minute. It's a fairy tale promoted by experienced bargainers to sucker unwary novices into accepting inferior deals.*

The simple fact is that the entire DZ (above Seller's MAP and below Buyer's MAP) can be seen as a bucket containing a specific number of dollars, which will be split between the two players. Each player strives to take home as many of these dollars as possible. The more dollars in the bucket, the fiercer the struggle. This isn't "win-win cooperation"; it's "win-lose competition." Every dollar gained by one player is a dollar not gained by his opponent. The struggle can be brutal, even ruthless. The stronger player takes home the biggest prize.

Inherited or Learned?

Some experienced bargainers claim their bargaining abilities are genetically transmitted, part of their "family genes".

That's hogwash. Nobody's "born" with bargaining ability. It's learned.

Many such boasters will have absorbed their bargaining tricks and techniques at an early age, from family and friends, in homes or early working endeavors. But meanwhile, other intelligent & competent individuals may spend their entire lifetimes never bargaining about anything at all, simply because their personal and professional environments don't require it.

For you, the reader, this may be a brand-new endeavor. But if you're still reading this book, you're demonstrating that you have a good work ethic, you're competent, you're intelligent, and you're willing to try something new.

Apply yourself to the task, and you can bargain with the best of them.

Who Is Your Opponent?

"Know Your Enemy"

This is basic military doctrine, followed by every leader from Alexander the Great to Norman Schwarzkopf, and it's applicable to every form of human competition, including bargaining.

Your Opponent's Goal

Your opponent's goal is to get as many of the DZ dollars as possible.

Within that DZ, whatever your opponent gets will be at your expense. The more your opponent gets, the less you get.

Since your opponent can't get any of those dollars if you drop out of the game, your sly opponent will try to leave you just barely enough of those dollars to keep you playing.

Your Opponent's Facade

Your opponent may try to get you to view these bargaining discussions as a happily cooperative endeavor in which he's "looking out for your interests" as well as his own.

> *Warning!*
> *Swallow this line, and I have a bridge in Brooklyn to sell you. Your opponent will never have your interests at heart. He's lulling you into a false sense of security to get you to let your guard down.*

A few years back I spent a somber afternoon walking through the Nazi death camp at Maidanek in southeastern Poland. The guards assured the Jewish prisoners that it was "for their own good" that they enter the "shower rooms" to "cleanse" themselves. Those guards then bolted the doors and turned on the gas. Be very suspicious of an opponent who offers you advice "for your own good."

Your opponent will spin the "win-win" bedtime story, emphasizing how lucky you are to take home some of the DZ dollars rather than going home with nothing at all. This is "win-win" only in the sense that each side ends up with something greater than nothing. Your opponent is trying to make you think that if you get anything greater than zero out of the deal, you should be happy and accept the result.

And your opponent will, of course, quietly downplay the fact that at the end of the day, he fully intends to sneak off with most of those dollars for himself.

I'll TAKE CARE OF YOU... TRUST ME!

Your Working Presumptions About Your Opponent

When assessing an opponent's capabilities and likely behavior, you start with a "worst-case" scenario of presumptions. These are the factors that (if correct) would give your opponent the greatest possible advantages over you in your current bargaining endeavor.

As you proceed, you may learn more about your opponent. To the extent that you're sure your information is accurate, you may choose to relax some of these working presumptions, one at a time. (Note, however, that these presumptions do indeed describe many real people. If you relax a presumption, just be sure you aren't giving in to wishful thinking.)

Your working presumptions about your opponent should always be

- that he's an experienced bargainer who has played this game many times before, and he's really good at it;

- that he's highly motivated, lean, and hungry;

- that he's well equipped with the latest hardware and software that gives him quick access to needed information;

- that he'll do everything he can to learn about your MAP, your ability to take a risk, and your ability to take your time;

- that he'll do everything he can to mislead you about his own MAP, his own ability to take a risk, and his own ability to take his time;

- that he'll abide by no ethical or moral constraints beyond those necessary to keep himself free of (civil or criminal) legal sanctions. In particular, that you can't count on him to keep a promise that he hasn't signed in writing.

The Key Principles of Bargaining

Four factors ultimately determine the end result of bargaining. They are

- Knowledge,

- Deception,

- Risk, and

- Time.

These factors will overlap and overshadow every step you take in the bargaining process. To bargain successfully, you need to have a continuing grasp of all four. Keep them always in mind. You will need to refer back to them over and over as you proceed through the bargaining process.

Knowledge

You're more likely to win a favorable deal to the extent that you acquire accurate knowledge about relevant facts and circumstances.

Deception

You're more likely to win a favorable deal to the extent that you (*legally*) prevent your opponent from acquiring accurate knowledge about relevant facts and circumstances.

Risk

You're more likely to win a favorable deal to the extent that you're able to take a risk.

How badly do you need this current deal? You're able to take a risk to the extent that your own business is strong enough to function well even if this current deal falls through. (See "What Is Risk?" discussed above.)

Time

You're more likely to win a favorable deal to the extent that you're able to take your time.

A player who's under time pressure to conclude a deal has to make more concessions than a player who isn't under such time pressure.

Strength and Weakness

The strength of a bargainer is determined by her ability to master and successfully utilize the four principles of knowledge, deception, risk, and time.

- A player's success in acquiring accurate knowledge and her success in deceiving her opponent are largely (but not totally) her own doing.

- A player's ability to take a risk and her ability to take her time may be largely (but not totally) beyond her own control.

In a matchup between two bargainers, their relative performances in mastering and successfully utilizing these four principles will ultimately determine the price at which they reach a deal.

> *Warning!*
> *Commentators here & there offer advice on "How to Bargain from a Position of Weakness". That's total hooey. There's no special trick to "bargaining from weakness".*

A player who lacks accurate knowledge, who cannot successfully deceive her opponent, who cannot take a risk, and who cannot take her time, will be at a disadvantage, no question about it. But there's no magic cure for this. You just have to buckle down and work hard at the four principles. This book shows you how to get the best possible price that's available to you under the circumstances. This book does *not* show you how to work magic.

Establishing and Maintaining a Reputation

Whether you bargain frequently or only just occasionally, your current endeavor won't be the only time you engage in bargaining. You can count on that.

Your opponent will take note of your tactics and your demeanor, your strengths and your weaknesses. And lots of very interested third parties will be watching, carefully but quietly, from the shadows. These people all talk to each other. The word gets around. You'll be bargaining again, some time, somewhere, with some of these people, about subjects unknown, in contexts unforeseen.

To the extent you've displayed any weaknesses in your bargaining posture, you can be sure your opponents will target those weaknesses the next time around.

- *Knowledge*—Have you prepared properly, done your due diligence, done your homework?

- *Deception*—Have you successfully concealed your MAP, your ability to take a risk, your ability to take your time? Can you control your mouth and your visible emotions?

- *And critically important*—Have you carefully heeded those many "warnings" that are sprinkled throughout this book?

> *Warning!*
> *When you're tired & weary, or pressed for time, or just unsure of yourself, it can be tempting to rationalize taking an easy out or cutting a corner "just this one time". You may tell yourself "this is just a little deal", or "this will never happen again", or "this isn't very important", or "I'll never see this player again", etc.*

Don't fall into this trap!

Cave in once, and the bargaining community smells blood. The word goes out that you're a pushover. This will make your own life far more difficult down the road.

Like it or not, what you do today establishes a precedent for what happens tomorrow.

You're never managing just that one subject that's currently on your plate. You're also building your own reputation. Take care to do it right, and it can pay handsome dividends in the future.

Why the Professors Don't Like This Book

It's because I tell the truth.

Deception: I tell the truth about the critical role of deception in bargaining, how to successfully practice deception yourself, and how to successfully defend against your opponent's deception.

Win-Lose: I tell the truth that final settlements on significant matters are almost always concluded on a win-lose basis.

The cold hard truths about Deception, and about Win-Lose, are the rules, not the exceptions, in bargaining.

The professors like the cloistered cocoon of the campus. They like to think that problems can always be resolved by cooperation and conciliation (guided, of course, by "intellectuals" such as themselves). They critique from the sidelines without having to live with the everyday consequences of their prescriptions. They squeamishly steer clear of competitive "Win-Lose" contests that involve "Deception". So they'll take every opportunity they can to disparage this book. Watch for them to do so. Listen to what they say. Compare it to this book. And make up your own mind.

OUR LEARNED PROFESSORS

PART III

The Critical Tools

Preparation Pays Off

In bargaining, as in so many other endeavors, good preparation can pay off big-time.

As Abe Lincoln once said, "If I had six hours to chop down a tree, I'd spend the first four sharpening my ax."

Get a Picture of What Lies Ahead

The first thing is to learn as much as possible about the agenda for this endeavor, what you'll encounter as you move ahead with this deal.

Nobody can predict the future flawlessly. But you should be able to make some educated estimates about the issues and the tasks, the markets and the politics, the events and the obstacles, that you're likely to encounter.

And you'll certainly need to identify and assess the personalities, the motivations, the working patterns, the strengths and the weaknesses, not only of your opponent(s), but also of any other persons who may play a part in this endeavor.

You're not likely to have at your fingertips all the information you'll need. But you have excellent sources of information all around you. Start with the internet, with its enormous amounts of information. Utilize available social networking channels. Don't overlook the print media, radio, TV, and your local libraries.

But above all, *talk to people*. Use your available contacts to approach anybody who may know something relevant to your deal, who may have had some experience in such endeavors, who may have some ideas about what you might run into. Many such individuals will be flattered you thought enough of their expertise to ask for their advice, and they'll often be happy to share some thoughts with you.

Probabilities and Priorities

For each item on the agenda, ask yourself:

- How important is it to my success? And

- How likely is it to happen?

A given item occupies a high place on your personal priority list to the extent that such item

- Is important to your success, and

- Appears likely to happen.

Set Your Stage

For each item, starting at the top of your priority list, identify the challenge(s) it will throw your way.

Think through what's needed to meet each such challenge.

Then round up and coordinate all the resources at your disposal to give yourself the maximum possible advantage in meeting this challenge successfully when it does arrive.

Roll Up Your Sleeves

Warning!
Preparation takes work. Sometimes it's drudge work. Sometimes it's dirty work.

This isn't just sitting behind a desk making plans. You'll have to walk the walk. You'll have to go places, to visit things, often to engage in manual labor.

Nobody will do this for you. You gotta get out there and do it on your own. You, and you alone, are the one who has to make things happen.

Remember the old Marine Corps proverb: "The more you sweat in peace, the less you bleed in war."

Manage Your Resources

Preparation inevitably requires an expenditure of some of your scarce resources. These resources can be your time, your money, your mental ability, your physical strength and energy, your emotional stamina, and your store of tangible physical assets.

Your resources may also include

- your store of favors that others owe to you, which you can call in as needed, and

- (last but not least) your own reputation.

Your own resources, like everyone's, are limited. This mandates prudence in their expenditure.

The amount of your scarce resources you should devote to any one deal is directly proportional to how much you have at stake in the matter. The more you stand to gain (or lose) in this endeavor, the more of your resources you should be willing to devote to it.

Watch for Moving Targets

Stay alert to what's changing on your bargaining horizon. Issues and tasks, markets and politics, events and obstacles, never stand completely still.

Change is continual. Most times it's evolutionary, more or less predictable. But sometimes it's sudden and unexpected.

Get ready to make midcourse corrections. You may have to do this when you least expect it.

The ground could be shifting under your feet. Be always prepared to take advantage of it. This is no time to rest on your laurels.

As Elbert Hubbard once said, "The only way to get away from opportunity is to lie down and die."

Know Yourself

Being objective about yourself and your own situation is difficult for anybody. Our emotions get in the way of our objectivity. But objectivity is vital to successful bargaining.

The following three factors can be reduced to, and expressed as, cold, hard, objective numbers, using data that's available to you. You must not only evaluate and determine these factors accurately, you must also acknowledge them emotionally.

- *Your own MAP*—This is the highest price you can pay and still make at least some money if you're a Buyer, the lowest price you can accept and still make at least some money if you're a Seller. It is *not* your estimate of what you think you might be able to get your opponent to agree to. And it's *not* something you're hoping for in your own dream world.

- *Your own ability to take a risk*—This is measured by how much you'll be damaged if your opponent decides to walk away and leave you high and dry without any deal at all. To the extent you're able to absorb such a downside result without being badly damaged, you're better able to take a risk. To the extent you'll be badly damaged by such a downside result, you're less able to take a risk.

- *Your own ability to take your time*—This is a little easier than establishing your MAP or your ability to take a risk. Your time deadlines are known to you. You just have to acknowledge them and learn to live with them.

Warning!
Safeguard the foregoing information with extreme care. If your opponent gets it, your hopes for a decent profit may go down the drain.

Study Your Opponent

Your perception of your opponent will color everything you do in this game. Gaining accurate knowledge about that individual is vital to your success.

It's also the most difficult single challenge you'll face, because she's doing everything she can to deceive you about the true nature of her situation.

Your task is to learn the truth about

- your opponent's MAP,

- your opponent's ability to take a risk, and

- your opponent's ability to take her time.

Your opponent's MAP is

- *if she's a Buyer*—The highest price she can pay and still make at least some money out of this deal. To what use can she put this Commodity if she buys if from you? Probe into everything you can find that may have a bearing on the market for such uses.

- *if she's a Seller*—The lowest price she can accept and still make at least some money out of this deal.

How feasible is it for her to use her resources to produce an alternative Commodity that she could sell to somebody else? Probe into everything you can find that may have a bearing on alternative uses for her resources.

Your opponent's ability to take a risk is measured by how much she'll be damaged if you decide to walk away and leave her high and dry without any deal at all:

- To the extent she's able to absorb such a downside result without being badly damaged, she's better able to take a risk.

- To the extent she'd be badly damaged by such a downside result, she's less able to take a risk.

Your opponent's ability to take her time is determined by the extent to which she has to:

- conclude this deal within an intrinsic time window that's necessary for the deal to be of value to her, and/or

- meet an external time deadline of any nature, and/or

- accommodate competing demands on her time.

Use your creative ingenuity to probe aggressively for any fact or circumstance that may have any relevance to your opponent's MAP or her ability to take a risk or her ability to take her time.

The key word here is *relevance*. Don't get sidetracked by seductive minutia that doesn't shed meaningful light on what you're looking for.

In order to gain accurate knowledge of a relevant fact or circumstance, you'll have to

- actively gather up all the raw data you can find that may have any bearing at all on what you're probing for,

- sift it for relevance, and

- put it into context to formulate an intelligent appraisal of how it may affect what you're looking for.

And don't overlook your opponent. You'd be surprised how often the best source of information about an opponent can be that opponent himself.

Gain his trust by finding some common ground to start a conversation. Probe for a favorite topic. Get him talking. (People love to talk about themselves.) Ask questions. Let him brag about his own history, his own achievements. Act ignorant and fascinated, and let him know you're really impressed. You may get him talking about his own priorities and deadlines, his own real needs.

It's easiest to do this in the "getting acquainted" stages, early in the game, at times and places when his guard is down.

Keep always uppermost in your mind that at every step of the game your opponent is doing everything within his power to deceive you about

- his MAP,

- his ability to take a risk, and

- his ability to take his time.

Remember always, *Eternal skepticism is the price of wisdom.*

Stay Alert for Relevant External Matters

Many other factors, both man-made and natural, can have a direct effect on the subject matter you're bargaining about. It's your task to keep your antenna proactively alert to any and all of them. Listen to the national and international news reports for items that may affect your own business endeavors. The following hypothetical examples may be illustrative:

- Unexpected weather causes major damage to the coffee crops in South America. This constricts the supply of coffee to international markets. Coffee prices rise astronomically. Worldwide coffee consumption falls. This may affect your decision about how much to offer for that gourmet coffee shop you're thinking about buying.

- American petroleum engineers figure out a way to get oil and gas out of rocks deep underground (called "fracking"). Worldwide oil production doubles and oil prices plummet. Places like Abu Dhabi and Venezuela that depend entirely on their oil production go into an economic tailspin. This may affect your decision on what to invest in those locations.

- A salmonella outbreak hits several California outlets of a national fast-food chain. Consumer panic causes that chain's sales to fall dramatically nationwide. This may affect your own decision on what price you can expect to get if you try to sell your own local franchise of that chain in your home state of New Jersey.

Control Your Mouth

Every time you make a good move in the bargaining game, you're gaining some dollars at your opponent's expense, dollars that he isn't getting. If you're successfully besting your opponent, he doesn't know how much you're really beating him by, how big a profit you're really making, and he's quite happy with his share of the money. Your path forward will be a whole lot rockier if he learns how many of those dollars may be slipping out of his grasp.

I once practiced law with a firm that occupied the top five floors (35 through 39) of a major office building in downtown Los Angeles. One afternoon, one of our attorneys entered the elevator on the 39th floor. It descended to 37, where two strangers got on. They began talking animatedly about how delighted they were to be settling their dispute for only $10 million, so glad their opponents didn't know they'd been willing to go as high as $85 million. Our lawyer kept a poker face on down to the ground floor, and when the strangers were out of sight, he promptly rode back up to 37 and asked the receptionist on that floor which of our attorneys those fellows had been talking to. This tale of the "elevator talk" still circulates in the lore of that distinguished firm.

"ELEVATOR TALK"

Throughout the entire bargaining process, you'll be communicating with many different people, about many different subjects, in many different contexts. Some will be your friends, some will be your enemies, and some will say they're your friends, but they're not. *It is critically important to watch what you say, when and where you say it, and to whom you say it.* In our age of electronic eavesdropping and hidden videotaping, you don't know who may be listening. Your default position should always be to assume that unfriendly ears are on the line.

Camouflage what you're doing. Don't tip your hand if there's any likelihood it could get to your opponent. Practice your poker face.

Take heed of that old wartime warning: "Loose lips sink ships."

The Critical Importance of "Face"

At the end of this deal, you want your opponent to walk away happy in the belief that he managed to win some really nice gains for himself. He may not know that you won a lot more than he did.

Never do anything that may cause him to "lose face" over this deal.

Warning!

One admonition that overshadows every-thing you do in this game is:

Never publicize a victory in bargaining.

Don't boast, Don't celebrate, Don't Gloat.

This goes both for interim little wins (like gaining a concession) and for big final victories at the end of the deal.

PUBLICIZING A VICTORY

It may be commonplace for an athlete to celebrate after scoring a touchdown or hitting a home run. In those games everybody knows he's done it, and there's no advantage in trying to keep it a secret. *But publicizing a win in bargaining can devastate you.* It can humiliate your opponent publicly, and there's never a stronger incentive for vindictive retribution:

- If you're midstream in the bargaining process, you'll find your opponent becomes much more difficult to deal with, perhaps even retracting some interim concessions he's already made.

- Even if you've already inked the deal, your opponent and his lawyers may examine the entire transaction with a microscope looking for reasons to justify unraveling it. (And those lawyers can be devilishly clever at such endeavors.)

At the very least, you will have made an enemy of your opponent, which can have far-reaching consequences:

- You may want to do business with this opponent again, in the future, on similar or unrelated endeavors. He won't be as hospitable next time.

- The word circulates throughout the neighborhood to other businessmen you may hope to deal with in the near or distant future. You may find them reluctant to do business with you, and/or more difficult to work with when they do.

- You could even become the target of an ambitious politician hoping to make an issue of your "obscene profits."

Your party-line for public consumption should be that you're making only a "modest" and "reasonable" profit from this deal.

Take your satisfaction from quietly sitting back and watching the growth of your own bank account, your own net worth, the price of your company's stock. *But keep your mouth shut*!

Working with Your Lawyers

Why Are Lawyers Important?

Like it or not, our business world is crisscrossed with a bewildering variety of legal rules and regulations. Venturing into this thicket without good legal advice is like walking blind into a minefield. It can be suicidal.

To bargain successfully, you need a lawyer in your corner. This is absolutely vital when you're dealing with matters of deception, whether generating such moves yourself or fielding them when they come from your opponent. (See the discussion below.)

> *Warning!*
> *Your opponent will definitely have a lawyer in his own corner. You can count on it. That lawyer may not always be visible at the bargaining table, but that lawyer will be there, behind the scenes.*

Finding A Suitable Lawyer

Lawyers of any caliber these days are specialists. You want to find one who's right for your needs. Word-of-mouth referrals are sometimes helpful, but the lawyer who got your neighbor's traffic ticket dismissed isn't necessarily the one to work with you on your business deal.

You can find excellent lawyer-search tools online. Two of the best-known directories are www.martindale.com and www.lawyers.com. Others are also available.

With these tools, you can quickly narrow down your lawyer search

- by geography (to your state, county, and city) and

- by category of legal specialization.

You'll find a wide variety of legal specializations listed in these directories. You won't usually find a separate one for "bargaining," but look for the subject matter you're dealing with, and a creative approach can narrow down your search pretty quickly.

In this way, you can come up with a short list of possibilities. Call and set up a brief introductory meeting with each one. Thirty minutes should be enough time to explain to them the nature of your inquiry and get from them an idea of what they can do for you, and their fee for doing so. (Some lawyers will charge you for this brief introductory meeting, while others will do it for free, but that shouldn't have much bearing on your decision of whom to hire.)

You can (but don't have to) be open with these candidates that these are recruiting interviews and that you're meeting with more than one lawyer. Prudence would suggest, however, that you not disclose to any candidate the names of the others to whom you're talking.

And finally, it can be advantageous to focus in on firms that have several lawyers practicing together (say, twelve or more). That way, if you hit on a novel issue that your favorite lawyer isn't familiar with, he may have a partner down the hall who's had some experience in that area.

How Your Lawyer Gets Paid

Your lawyer's time and advice are one of your key resources. As pointed out above, the amount of this (and other) resources you devote to a deal is directly proportional to how much you stand to gain (or lose) in the matter.

Your lawyer will bill you for the time he spends working on your legal matters. He keeps detailed records of his time for billing purposes. This explains a lot about his behavior. If you chat with him on the telephone, or if you meet with him at his office, or even if you're having drinks with him after work, whenever you're talking about your legal matters, your lawyer's meter is running, and you'll get billed for it. So don't expect to drop by casually to discuss your legal matters without paying for it.

A good lawyer is an educated and competent professional. His fees reflect this. They'll start around $200 an hour and go north from there. Live with it. This isn't the place to cut corners. You get what you pay for.

The Flavor of the Legal Profession

The profession as a whole has a reputation that can be less than savory. That reputation is often justified. However, it's decidedly unwise to squeeze the lawyers out of your game plan for that reason. Understanding the motivations that make lawyers act the way they do (and that indeed make the entire legal profession tick) can give you a major advantage in weaving your own lawyer into the picture as one of your most important resources.

- *A lawyer's public image is extraordinarily important to her.* Absent a clear-cut litigation victory (which doesn't happen very often), it can be difficult for a client to evaluate a lawyer's work. For this reason, a lawyer takes great pains to project an outward public appearance of polished professional competence, impeccable ethical integrity, and (of course) personal financial success. To a much-greater degree than other professions, a lawyer's reputation and her standing in the community are money in the bank for her. She will buttress her professional image with whatever degrees, credentials, and other status symbols she can amass for herself. But don't be too fooled by that Rolex and that Mercedes, which can be marketing props designed to create the impression that (a) she's financially successful, and therefore (b) she must be a really good lawyer, and therefore (c) you should hire her. (In reality, she may barely be squeezing out the monthly payments on those items.) And she will, of course, utilize some extraordinarily clever verbal smokescreens not only to convince her client that she's doing a great job for that client, but also to cover her backside when she makes a mistake.

- *Lawyers are trained to focus more on problems than on solutions.* Starting her first day in law school and continuing on through the bar exam, the fledging lawyer encounters a strong professional emphasis on identifying and highlighting problems, far more than on crafting solutions to them. This mind-set inevitably carries over into her career practices. When she encounters a new situation, her immediate knee-jerk reaction is to look for what's wrong in the picture and criticize it, rather than pointing out what's right and helping it grow. This doesn't sit well with the client who may be trying to build or create something and who wants legal advice to show him the steps he can take to accomplish this, rather than the reasons why he can't.

- *Lawyers can be cleverly deceptive with their language.* The fabric of a lawyer's stock in trade is her skill in manipulating the English language to serve the ends of her client (and/or herself). A good lawyer is adept at using words to make things appear different than they really are. This ability is useful when cross-examining a witness in court or arguing a delicate point of law, but its constant use can impede a lawyer's ability to grasp and appreciate everyday objective truth. (Lawyers never admit they lie about anything, they just "prevaricate" or "dissemble" or "equivocate." Look up those terms in your dictionary, and you'll see what I mean about manipulating the language.)

- *And lawyers are, of course, notoriously argumentative.* Because that's what they do all day, every day. Say "good morning" to a lawyer, and she'll often find a reason to contend that the morning isn't really all that good.

The good news is that the foregoing doesn't describe all lawyers. Such attitudes and behavior patterns may be widespread within the profession, but there are lots and lots of exceptions. Do a little digging, and you can find many lawyers who are genuinely decent people.

Ground Rules For Using A Lawyer

Your lawyer works for you, not vice versa. Make this clear at the outset, politely but quite firmly. Many a lawyer assumes that as soon as she's been retained, she's free to start ordering her client around. That's not acceptable. You've hired her, you're paying her, so you're in the driver's seat.

Insist that she communicate with you in plain English that you can understand, using language that answers your questions and meets your needs. The legal profession has long been notorious for using confusing language to express straightforward thoughts. This serves nobody's interest but those of that profession, and you needn't put up with it. To be sure, the profession has made some strides in recent years in improving its usage of English. However, if your lawyer strays over into excessive legalese, you shouldn't hesitate to rein her in and make her repeat things in language you can understand. And whenever you feel it's necessary, you should likewise insist that she translate for you any documentation you receive from your opponent's lawyer.

Make it clear that your lawyer's task is to craft solutions to your problems, not just to identify the obstacles in your path or the reasons why something can't be done. This may take a sea change in the traditional thought patterns of many lawyers, but it can be done if you insist on it. Get your lawyer thinking and talking in terms of accomplishing your goals.

At every step of the way, get a clear understanding of just exactly what your lawyer is going to do, why she's doing it, and how much it will cost you. Giving her a blank check is a recipe for disaster. Keep her on a leash, follow up on her work, and monitor what she does for you. Ask for periodic updates, as necessary.

Make a practice of getting your lawyer into the picture early on, in whatever you're doing. A little bit of legal input in the planning stages of an endeavor can save you lots of money and lots of headaches in the long run. (The fictional "consigliere" in *The Godfather* may generate some food for thought.)

Don't withhold information from your lawyer. Matters that seem insignificant to you may be quite important legally. Your lawyer does have a professional obligation to keep your information confidential, and lawyers are generally pretty good about honoring this requirement. Familiarizing your lawyer with your business will facilitate her ability to give you good advice.

If you're uneasy with your lawyer's advice, you can get a second opinion. The above discussion on "Finding a Suitable Lawyer" makes it quick and easy to find and interview new lawyers. Having gone through that exercise once, you may already have a short list. But take care to handle this with kid gloves. It's not wise to let your first lawyer know that you're seeking a second opinion. And there's no need to disclose your first lawyer's identity to your second lawyer. You will, of course, pay your second lawyer for her advice.

If you're dissatisfied with your lawyer, you can replace her. Be sure to sugarcoat this move, tactfully and politely, with the lawyer you're leaving. Lawyers can be vindictive. Don't make an enemy when you don't have to. (And there's always the possibility you might want to go back to her someday.)

And if you're happy with your lawyer, tell the world about it. This kind of publicity not only strokes her ego; it fuels her bank account, and it may charge her up to go some extra miles for you.

The Hidden Secret to Getting the Best Legal Advice

When bargaining, you'll have to make important choices about alternatives that entail some legal risk. These risks may be legal challenges from your opponent or other parties, and/or possible civil (or even criminal) penalties from governmental authorities.

In such cases, the law won't give you easy yes-or-no answers to guide your decision-making. You'll be operating in the legally delicate "gray areas".

Guidance from the right lawyer can be worth his weight in gold to you in these gray areas, provided that

- you've chosen him carefully, he's good at his calling, you've clued him into the picture on your business activities, and you trust him; *and*

- you discuss your options with him quietly and orally, in confidence and in private, off the record, unwritten, unrecorded, and (if need be) unwitnessed.

Anything you say to your lawyer in these conversations will be covered by the "attorney-client privilege," which means that your lawyer is ethically prohibited from disclosing anything you say to him, unless you consent to it.

However, this privilege does *not* run both ways. There's no legal rule against a client's disclosing what advice his lawyer gave to him. Your lawyer's greatest nightmare is the damage to his professional reputation that could result if it became *publicly* known that he gave legal advice that ended up harming a client. This would subject him not only to open ridicule from his professional competitors, but (far more important) to serious erosion of that carefully crafted public image that fuels his bank account.

Therefore, you should go out of your way to commit to your lawyer and to reassure him over and over, as often as necessary, that you will keep his communications to you every bit as confidential as he is obliged to keep your communications to him.

Of course, nobody should ever tell a lie about what goes on in such conversations. And your attorney, being of impeccable ethical integrity, would never, ever, dream of doing so. But keeping such conversations quiet and oral, confidential, private, off the record, unwritten, unrecorded, and unwitnessed has been known to provide the occasional opportunity for a convenient bout of amnesia. (Politicians routinely refer to this as "plausible deniability.")

This gives your lawyer the greatest possible leeway to offer fully candid advice to you about the pros and cons, the strengths and weaknesses of your possible alternative courses of action in those legal "gray areas."

Making Your Decisions

Your trusted lawyer has analyzed your situation, and he has given you his best professional assessment of your legal risks. You have paid him handsomely for his service. At this point, he departs the picture.

You're now on your own. You have to examine all relevant factors carefully and make your own intelligently thought-out choices on which of those legal risks you are, and are not, prepared to undertake. It's up to you.

Warning!
Your lawyer isn't your equity partner. He won't share with you any of the fruits of your business successes. You shouldn't expect him to shoulder any of the down-sides, either. His advice doesn't inoculate you against bad news.

If things turn sour and you're unhappy (after the fact) with his services, your remedy is to get a new lawyer for your future endeavors.

Don't be too quick to publicize any unhappiness with your previous lawyer. And forget about suing for legal malprac-tice. Try to pass the buck that way and it spreads to the other lawyers in town. And you run out of lawyers, real fast.

Fooling Your Opponent

The Role of (Legal) Deception

Deception is accepted as a key element in most competitive endeavors, more prominent in some than others.

- In football, a quarterback doesn't come out of the huddle and tell the opposing team what play he's going to run; he strives to fool them by doing something unexpected.

- In draw poker, you don't display your hand to your opponent; you bluff to try to get him to either bet more than he should, or fold and concede.

Bargaining is no different. Deception (within the limits of the law) is an accepted part of the game.

WASHINGTON DECEIVES THE BRITISH

For some of the best guidelines on deception, we can look at that ultimate form of competition, namely warfare. We, of course, don't engage in violence, and we also realize that we must keep our opponent in the game by conceding to him at least some of the Deal Zone. But we can benefit from some thoughts of those who have observed, practiced, and written about the subject of war:

- Recall the wisdom of Sun Tzu, the influential Chinese philosopher who wrote many centuries ago that "All warfare is based on deception. When you are strong, make the enemy think you are weak. When you are near, make the enemy think you are far."

- And we need look no further than George Washington's masterful uses of deception when he snuck in cannons and expelled the British from Boston, when he crossed the Delaware River in the dead of night and defeated the surprised Hessians at dawn, and when he fooled the British spyglasses by keeping a skeleton crew at West Point while he marched his entire army south to our final victory at Yorktown.

The Structure of Deception

Your opponent, like you, is doing everything he can to try to gain accurate knowledge about you and about other facts and circumstances relevant to the subject matter at hand.

Your task is to use all available (*legal*) means to prevent your opponent from gaining information that could give him any insight into:

- *Your own MAP.* This is the highest price you can pay and still make at least some money if you're the Buyer, the lowest price you can accept and still make at least some money if you're the Seller.

  ◆ *If you're the Buyer.* Any information on the use to which you can put this Commodity if you buy it from your opponent. Think about anything your opponent could find bearing on the market for such uses.

  ◆ *If you're the Seller.* Any information on how feasible it would be for you to use your resources to produce an alternative Commodity that you could sell to somebody else. Probe into everything you can find that may have a bearing on alternative uses for your opponent's resources.

- *Your own ability to take a risk.* This is measured by how much you'd be damaged if your opponent were to walk away and leave you high and dry without any deal at all.

- *Your own ability to take your time.* This is determined by the extent to which you have to:

  ◆ conclude this deal within a time window necessary for the deal to be of value to yourself, and/or

  ◆ meet an external time deadline of any nature, and/or

  ◆ accommodate competing demands on your time.

To the extent you can do so, you also want to use all available (*legal*) means to prevent your opponent from gaining accurate information about any "relevant external matters"

(discussed above) that could affect the subject matter of your bargaining.

Some Guidelines on Deception

Deceive your opponent about any relevant fact or circumstance to the extent (and only to the extent) that

- you have knowledge of that fact or circumstance and

- your opponent lacks knowledge of that fact or circumstance.

Keeping passively silent about "inside information" that could help your opponent can be just as effective (but just as risky) as actively deceiving her about it.

Regarding deceptive language:

- A "generally worded" communication (which can later be "interpreted" or "clarified") is preferable to a precisely worded "specific" communication.

- An oral communication is preferable to a written communication. (One who makes an oral statement can easily develop a short memory and later forget what he had said.)

- An unwitnessed oral communication is obviously preferable to a witnessed oral communication.

Face-to-Face Theatrics

Successful deception will require you to convincingly communicate to your opponent, in person, the message you want her to absorb.

Such play-acting can be the keystone of your program of deception. Learn it well. Practice how to respond to your opponent's offer. Slap yourself on the forehead, roll your eyes, throw up your arms, moan loudly in agony.

Earn yourself an Academy Award.

Actors aren't the only ones who do this. Lawyers do it all the time. So do most politicians. Now it's your turn.

The Importance of Your Lawyer

The steps you can take to deprive your opponent of accurate information cover a wide spectrum, all the way from actions that are considered acceptably normal behavior to actions that are clearly unacceptable and that risk drawing civil (and even criminal) sanctions. In between the red and green lights at either end of the spectrum, there are many shades of gray. *This is where you really need legal counsel.*

Look at examples from the opposite ends of the spectrum:

- You're the Buyer responding to the Seller's price quotation. You groan pitifully and state, "There's just no way I could pay a price that high and stay in business." Your statement is false. You could indeed pay the quoted price and still make a decent profit, but you hope to get him to lower his price further. Your rhetoric hasn't violated any legal or ethical rule, and it's considered standard give-and-take in the bargaining process.

- You're the Seller offering your ongoing business for sale. You give the Buyer a false set of financial statements that make the business look a lot more profit-

92

able than it really is. This is a clear violation of both ethical and legal rules against such behavior, and it could open you up to civil (and even criminal) penalties.

So I repeat here again, with emphasis, the following Starting Assumption:

Each player works closely with his lawyer at every step of the game, hence carefully avoids doing anything that could lead to civil or criminal penalties.

You and Your Conscience

Does the idea of "deceiving" somebody bother you? Do you suspect that your personal sense of ethics and morality may hold you to a standard "higher" than that of "mere compliance with the law"?

Remember the game you're playing. If you're reading this book, you're in business. You're dealing with an opponent who is a tough, seasoned bargainer, who'll use any opportunity to take full advantage of you every chance he gets.

Should you ever find yourself dealing with widows and orphans, you'll be in a different ball game. Obviously, you don't take unfair advantage of them. But that's not what this book is about. Your Bible can be your guide for widows and orphans, but the book you're now reading is your guide for business.

Making A Concession

The Critical Role of Reciprocating Concessions

Making visible concessions is an indispensable component of successful bargaining.

The structure of bargaining is a back-and-forth pattern of offer, followed by rejection and counteroffer, followed by another rejection and counteroffer, etc., until the parties either reach a mutually satisfactory deal or terminate the bargaining process.

A player's counteroffer inevitably embodies a retreat (a "concession") from that player's previous offer. Doing it right is crucial to successful bargaining.

It's critical to note that many experienced bargainers (whether Sellers or Buyers) won't even deal with someone who refuses to engage in the time-honored back-and-forth ritual described in this book, even if that means forfeiting a share of the dollars in the DZ.

This isn't just a matter of egos and personal pride. A bargainer's reputation within the bargaining community is an extremely valuable asset for that individual, and it's very much at stake in such instances.

Players who don't budge from their initial offers, and assume a take-it-or-leave-it posture, can find huge chunks of their potential markets evaporating.

(Indeed, US courts have ruled that in labor-management contract discussions, an employer or a union that refuses to make any concession from its initial position has thereby committed an "unfair labor practice," which can carry heavy penalties under federal law.)

A Bargaining Concession Is Not A "Win-Win" Move

A properly executed bargaining concession is a tool to help you gain the best possible price for yourself. It's not a friendly giveaway. You've progressed far beyond the "Win-Win" stage. You're now in the "Win-Lose" mode of the Deal Zone, and you're working with the four principles of Knowledge, Deception, Risk and Time.

An inexperienced player who lacks the stomach, or the will, or the energy, to persevere in his own interest may slip into the emotional trap of thinking of a contemplated concession as "Win-Win" generosity, in the hope that his opponent will reciprocate in kind. This is wishful thinking. A competent opponent will do no such thing. Cave in to this once and your opponent will expect more such "generosity" from you, over and over.

Smile for the camera. Act visibly and outwardly courteous to everyone. But don't fool yourself. Don't expect this performance to do anything *for you* other than soften up your opponent.

Remember the wisdom of Leo Durocher: *"Nice guys finish last."*

Managing Your Concessions

Any rejection you make, followed by a retreating counter-offer on your part, can constitute an inherent threat to your entire posture in the bargaining process.

The threat is greater to the extent that your retreating counteroffer is distant from

- your initial offer/counteroffer, and/or

- your immediately preceding counteroffer.

In any such case, you will be faced with three distinct tasks:

- To establish and maintain the legitimacy of your immediately preceding offer / counteroffer, and

- To justify your retreat from that immediately preceding offer / counteroffer, and

- (Totally aside from the foregoing) To establish an independent legitimacy for your new counteroffer.

Successfully accomplishing these tasks will be among the biggest challenges a bargainer faces. There'll be an enormous variety of contexts, hence there is no one-size-fits-all solution. Having said that, however, a prudently creative and aggressive approach using the principles of Knowledge, Deception, Risk, and Time can bring success in these endeavors.

Some tactics that may be helpful in justifying your retreat from your immediately preceding offer/counteroffer are:

- Demand an identifiable concession in return. ("No free lunch!" is the refrain.) This can take the form of

(a) asking for something new from your opponent or (b) retracting something from your previous offer.

- Moan long and loud about how much this concession hurts you. Here's where you use your well-rehearsed theatrics. Slap yourself on the forehead, roll your eyes, throw up your arms, moan loudly in agony.

- Get up on your moral high horse and make your opponent feel painfully guilty or ashamed for having done this terrible thing to you. (See the discussion in "Face-to-Face Theatrics" above.)

- Lay prominent claim to an unspecified future concession from your opponent. ("You owe me one" is the refrain.)

Insist On A Responsive Counteroffer

Once you've made an offer/counteroffer, you should *never* consider retreating further from that position until and unless your opponent first extends a responsive counteroffer of his own.

> *Warning!*
> *Many a slickster will try to get something for nothing by asking you to make another concession before that person puts a counteroffer on the table. Some of the refrains might be. "That's not good enough" / "You can do better than that" / "Give me something I can work with."*

Don't fall for this trap. Once you've extended an offer/counteroffer, the ball's in your opponent's court, and you're entitled to a responsive counteroffer before you proceed any further.

Give in to such a ploy just once, and you not only forfeit any leverage you may have with this opponent, you can do irreparable damage to your own reputation within the bargaining community.

If your opponent persists in refusing to put a legitimately responsive counteroffer on the table, you should be fully prepared to terminate the bargaining and move on to other endeavors. (And a credible threat to do just that will usually get an opponent to come around with a responsive counteroffer.)

Multiple Concessions

You will often have to make successive concessions as you proceed with the back-and-forth of bargaining.

Your first concession will normally be your largest, and your follow-on concessions in progressively smaller increments.

This approach strengthens the legitimacy of your overall posture and strongly suggests to your opponent that you're approaching your MAP.

Bargaining Isn't Poker

Don't ever confuse bargaining with poker.

A naïve novice may see bargaining as just another form of poker. The similarities are that both games consist of a series of back-&-forth moves. Each player has some assets in his corner, and his success is determined largely by his ability to fool his opponent about the size and strength of those assets.

But that's where the similarity ends.

Poker is a winner-take-all endeavor where you win big if you scare your opponent into dropping out of the game.

Bargaining is a shared-pot endeavor where you lose everything if you scare your opponent into dropping out of the game.

You *must* keep your opponent in the game, and the way to do this is to see that he gets a share of the profits that he finds acceptable.

If your opponent doesn't win something, you don't win anything.

Make Sure Your Opponent Scores Some Wins

If you're doing things right, you're in the driver's seat, you're controlling the game. Good for you.

But don't ever forget that your opponent is also in this game to make money. If he ever drops out, you'll be left high and dry with nothing. So be very careful to keep him in the game. The way to do this is to let him win some money.

If this is a one-time deal, you need only let him win just enough to keep him in the game.

But if you're contemplating future deals with this player, you may want to let him win more than that minimum. The amount will be up to your judgment. There's no set formula; every case is different.

But stay in the driver's seat.

And if (contrary to the guidelines in this book) he wants to boast openly about his "successes," let him do so. It makes it less likely that he'll want to go back and change anything.

Points and Ranges

Novice bargainers will sometimes express an offer or a counteroffer as a "range." (For example, a Seller may tell a Buyer that the Seller is "looking to get between $80,000 and $100,000" for whatever he's selling.)

This is hopelessly naive. The opponent will hear only the end point of that range that's most favorable to that opponent, and all of the discussions will start from there.

Successful bargainers state their offers and counteroffers as points, not ranges.

Speedups and Slowdowns

Speedups

If your opponent is trying to speed up the bargaining process without any visibly legitimate reason, it usually means that

- she thinks she's ahead of you in the processes of acquiring knowledge for herself and of preventing you from acquiring knowledge for yourself, and she wants to prod you into making a quick commitment before you catch up to her; and/or

- she's under time pressure to conclude a deal quickly.

In either case, the passage of time works in your favor:

- Do whatever you can to delay the process and drag things out while you apply yourself to acquiring more and more relevant knowledge.

- And if you do decide to acquiesce and speed things up, make your opponent pay with any and all concessions that may be available.

Slowdowns

If your opponent is trying to slow down the bargaining process without any visibly legitimate reason, it usually means that

- she thinks she's behind you in the processes of acquiring knowledge for herself and of preventing you from acquiring knowledge for yourself, and she wants to buy time to catch up to you; and/or

- she's able to take her time, and she thinks you're under time pressure to conclude a deal quickly; and/or

- she's stalling to explore other business opportunities of some nature.

In any of the above cases, the passage of time may be working against you:

- Do whatever you can to speed up the process.

- And if you do decide to acquiesce in her delays, make her pay with any and all concessions that may be available.

Protracted Bargaining

As Time Drags On

The foregoing analyses assume that the back-and-forth of bargaining will be completed within a reasonably compacted period of time, at the end of which the parties will either reach an agreement on price, or terminate the talks and go their separate ways.

But situations do arise where the communications go on and on for extended periods of time, without much rapid progress toward a conclusion. Sometimes this results from the inherent nature of the subject matter, sometimes from the deliberate action of one (or both) of the players.

When the discussions are protracted in this manner, two major considerations become overridingly important for any player. These are (a) the limitations on that player's available time and (b) the ongoing drain on that player's other resources.

The Limitations on Available Time

Time is one of the four principles of bargaining enumerated earlier in this book.

A given player is more likely to win a favorable deal to the extent that he's able to take his time.

And he's under more pressure to make concessions to the extent that he needs to complete a deal before a time deadline.

The Ongoing Drain on Other Resources

Besides time, the other resources available to a given player are finite. They may include his money, his other tangible physical assets, and his store of favors that others owe to him. They may include his mental and physical strength and energy, and his emotional stamina. And they may also include (last but not least) his own personal reputation.

As long as the bargaining continues without a resolution, these resources will be focused on the subject matter at hand. They will be unavailable for other endeavors, and they will be drained, bit by bit, as time continues to pass.

Keeping these resources out of play inevitably entails an "opportunity cost". The Commodity a player is bargaining about isn't the only business option available to him. Alternative prospects pop up continuously on the horizon, many of which can be quite attractive.

Some of these alternatives will pop up unexpectedly, midstream in a player's then-current bargaining endeavor, which can cause him to seriously consider a mid-course correction. Is he better off continuing to devote his limited resources to this time-consuming venture, or should he make a concession big enough to speed up progress toward a deal, or should he pull out from this endeavor entirely and put his resources to better use elsewhere?

As time passes, any given player will be less and less willing to devote his time and resources to this endeavor. This isn't just a game of "chicken", pitting one ego against another. It's a matter of cold, hard calculations of risk and reward, of costs and benefits, of when and where and how to allocate your scarce resources in order to achieve the best possible result for yourself.

Breaking the Logjam

In the event of an impasse, any player has the option of either

- making a concession to (hopefully) speed up the bargaining progress in the direction of a deal, or

- terminating the talks and pulling out to pursue other opportunities elsewhere.

The players' relative capabilities with the principles of Knowledge, Deception, Risk, and Time come directly into play at this juncture. (See the discussion on Strength and Weakness, above.)

- A player who perceives her vulnerability to protracted bargaining to be greater than her opponent's will become, over time, more and more willing to make bigger and bigger concessions if she wants to close the deal.

- A player who perceives her vulnerability to protracted bargaining to be less than her opponent's may become, over time, progressively stingier in her concessions. Indeed, she may sometimes even reverse direction by making a new demand, or otherwise pushing her offer farther from her MAP than it had been.

Sunk Costs

Warning!
Sunk costs are irrelevant.

This MBA truism means quite simply that at any given point in time, a player has at his disposal a finite amount of resources, and he confronts a given array of opportunities. The guideline for his decision-making should be how best to employ those existing resources, in pursuit of those existing opportunities, so as to gain the best likelihood of future success.

He may have expended resources in a past endeavor that hasn't (yet) produced his desired results. If the potential future gain from that past endeavor doesn't match the potential from a newer prospect now on his horizon, he should bring his limited resources to bear the one offering the best likelihood of success. He shouldn't feel tied to the earlier endeavor.

A clear-eyed businessman thinks in terms of today and tomorrow, not the past. He thinks forward to his potential future profits and losses, not backward at his historical balance sheet. Throwing good money after bad never makes sense.

- But not all such bargainers are sensible. Some feel emotionally obligated to "justify" their previous expenditures by staying on their earlier path. This is irrational, but many people do it. It seems to be human nature.

- And not all bargainers are working for themselves or on their own. Many a bargainer has an audience of bosses or other constituents who are quite likely to penalize him if he doesn't stay on his original course and bring that endeavor through to some sort of a conclusion.

Such vulnerable players will become easier prey late in the game, as they approach their time deadlines. A savvy opponent will watch for this and take advantage of it.

The Walkout

What Is A Walkout?

(in response to an offer from your opponent) Discontinuing the bargaining talks and physically leaving the premises.

When you walk out, you give any arguably credible excuse as your reason for doing so (e.g., "I need to check on a few things," etc.).

Walking out

- lets you step back to assess your opponent's offer in order to better formulate a response,

- buys you some time to investigate matters relevant to your position,

- buys you time to improve your deception of your opponent,

- gives you a chance to explore other money-making options that may be available to you,

"THE WALKOUT"

- makes your opponent *worry* that you're exploring other options (which worry can be magnified to the extent that you haven't set a date and time for reconvening), and/or

- eats up time, when you can afford to take it and your opponent can't.

The Defensive Walkout

A walkout executed *before* rejecting or accepting your opponent's offer.

Your default line for the defensive walkout is "I'll have to give the matter some thought."

The defensive walkout doesn't expressly terminate the bargaining discussions and leaves the door open for you to reconnect with your opponent later at some (unspecified) later time.

You "reassure" your opponent with the refrain that "I'll get back to you." This keeps the ball in your court (and of course, it doesn't "reassure" your opponent very much at all).

The defensive walkout is especially useful when your primary motivation is to stop and get your bearings.

The Offensive Walkout

A walkout executed *after* rejecting your opponent's offer but *without* making any counteroffer.

Your default line for the offensive walkout is "No, I'm afraid that really won't work at all. If you'll excuse me, I have another appointment to go to right now. Don't call me. I'll call you."

The offensive walkout leaves your opponent fearful that you're on the verge of terminating the bargaining discussions and leaving him high and dry, without any deal at all.

The offensive walkout is especially useful when your primary motivation is to rattle your opponent.

Some Guidelines on Walking Out

The Walkout can be most effective late in the game, after your opponent has invested considerable time and resources in the bargaining, doesn't want to see all his efforts go down the drain, and may be more amenable to making further concessions.

The Walkout can be most effective if, at the time of the walkout, you *don't* set a date and time for reconvening.

Among experienced bargainers, it's usually considered *"de rigeur"* to walk out at least once in every bargaining endeavor.

PART IV

Step By Step in Practice

The following is a chronological checklist to guide you in proceeding through the bargaining process.

You're On Stage!

From the very beginning to the very end of your bargaining endeavor, you're on visible display and you're playing a role.

Everything you say and do, and all aspects of your personal appearance and demeanor, should be designed to deliver your message *credibly* to your opponent. So put on your acting shoes and step into the limelight!

Your clothing and your grooming are important. But far beyond those, pay special attention to your speech and voice, your posture, your body language, your mannerisms.

Ever been to Disneyland? The young man in the Mickey Mouse costume is rarely a professional actor, usually just a student with minimal coaching putting himself through college. But while he's out there "onstage," he's mingling with the crowd and enchanting the visitors.

You may not be accustomed to play-acting, but if you're serious about bargaining, you can learn to do this. It's not all that difficult. You don't have to change your personality. Practice acting out your role in front of a mirror at home. Practice with a trusted friend or relative. You'll get it right.

Image is critical. Look the part, act the part, talk the part, be the part!

Stay Focused

Your goal is to get the best possible price for yourself. This is purely a moneymaking business endeavor, nothing more.

To achieve your objective, it's imperative that you remain focused on the dollars-and-cents factors that are the most powerful in getting you to where you want to be.

Your opponent will not only attempt to deceive you about his MAP, his ability to take his time, and his ability to take a risk, he may also throw a variety of other distractions at you, with the aim of diverting your attention, your energy, your time, and your other resources, away from the real task at hand.

- He may try to discourage you by dropping disparaging personal comments about your ability, your character, your personal history, or anything else that could deflate your ego and your will to proceed.

- He may try to anger you, to sucker you into making an ill-advised retaliatory move.

Such tactics all have in common the aim of taking your mind off your goal, of distracting you from the real issues you're dealing with.

STAY FOCUSED

I recently watched a pro football game featuring a home-team player with an explosively hot temper. The score was close, and late in the game a visiting player gave that home-team player a little bump and muttered something under his breath, unnoticed by the crowd or the referees. The hot-tempered player responded by grabbing that visiting player and throwing him to the ground, in full view of the crowd and the TV cameras. The referees assessed his team a major penalty for unsportsmanlike conduct, which cost them the game and a chance to play in the Super Bowl. (The player who baited him wasn't penalized.)

The lesson from this is to remain coolheaded and professional. Rein in your emotions. Stay focused on your goal.

Determine Whether the Situation Calls for Bargaining

Commodities are bought and sold as either

- "Set Price" transactions (a can of beans at your local supermarket) or

- "Bargained Price" transactions (a parcel of real estate or an ongoing business operation).

With a quick glance, you can usually see which type of transaction you're facing. But not always.

Some situations are ambiguous. This can be especially important if your opponent is the one who makes the first offer. In such cases, what posture should you take?

If the situation is set-price, and you try to bargain, you'll usually be corrected promptly. You may waste a little time and energy, but nothing worse.

On the other hand, if the situation calls for bargaining and you approach it as set-price, you'll either

- accept your opponent's (initial) offer and give away the store or

- reject your opponent's offer and walk away from a potentially profitable deal.

Either way, you'll lose.

Therefore, when in doubt, the best default position is to presume that the situation calls for bargaining, and proceed down that path until and unless that presumption is disproved.

The Critical Importance of MAP

The single most important factor to keep uppermost in your mind, at all times and above all else, is MAP.

Why? Because the distance between MAP and the sale price is profit, both for you and for your opponent.

Guard your own MAP, your break-even price, below which you (as a seller) cannot sell profitably, above which you (as a buyer) cannot buy profitably. You should never do or say anything that gives even the slightest hint of your own MAP. That includes celebrating a "good deal". Your opponent will be watching, waiting, listening.

Learn everything you can about your opponent's MAP. He knows (and you know) that if you locate the vicinity of his MAP you will gain a tremendous bargaining advantage over him. He'll do everything he can to conceal his MAP from you. And you should do everything in your power to learn about his MAP.

Examine Your Starting Assumptions

The "Starting Assumptions" identified earlier in this book are the keys to highlighting the critical factors that make for success in bargaining

In the real world, however, it's not unusual to encounter a deviation from one or more of these Starting Assumptions.

Therefore, in order to come properly to grips with the situation at hand you must address these Starting Assumptions and assess the extent to which each one may (or may not) apply to your case.

For example, is your opponent pursuing one or more secondary objectives, in addition to (or in lieu of) the presumed primary objective of getting the best possible price? Is that person motivated by sweetheart deals, back-door kickbacks, or other ulterior motives?

To the extent the situation at hand relaxes any given Starting Assumption, you must overlay that factor onto your plans for this particular endeavor.

Remember, every deal is different in its own way. There's never any substitute for an intelligent analysis of the idiosyncrasies of each case.

Do Your Homework

These factors have been stated above, but they're important enough to reemphasize here.

Know Yourself

Identify your MAP.

Your MAP is the worst-case scenario of the rock-bottom dollar quantity you'd be willing to settle for if worse comes to worst, without walking away from this deal entirely and permanently.

Your MAP *must* be a clearly defined single point. It is *never* a "range" that you're emotionally "shooting for" based on your shrewdly considered assessment of what you might possibly be able to squeeze out of this deal.

Identifying your own MAP requires a cold, hard, emotionless assessment of reality, and this isn't always easy.

Emotionally and psychologically, *identifying your own map can be half the ball game.*

Acknowledge your ability to take a risk.

HOMEWORK

This is measured by how much you'll be damaged if your opponent decides to walk away and leave you high and dry without any deal at all. To the extent you're able to absorb such a downside result without being badly damaged, you're better able to take a risk. To the extent you'll be badly damaged by such a downside result, you're less able to take a risk.

Acknowledge your ability to take your time:

Examine carefully

- any intrinsic/inherent time window within which you have to conclude this deal in order for the deal to be of value to you,

- any extrinsic/externally generated deadline you're facing,

- any competing demands on your time,

- etc.

Study Your Opponent

Your task is to learn the truth about

- your opponent's MAP,

- your opponent's ability to take a risk, and

- your opponent's ability to take his time.

Use your creative ingenuity to probe aggressively for any fact or circumstance that may have any relevance to your opponent's MAP or his ability to take a risk or his ability to take his time.

Don't overlook your opponent. You'd be surprised how often the best source of information about an opponent can be that opponent himself.

Remember, *Eternal skepticism is the price of wisdom.*

Study Anything Else That's Relevant

Many other factors can have a direct effect on the subject matter you're bargaining about.

I was once extricating a client from a long-term lease on an industrial building in a Midwestern city. Under that lease my client had financial responsibility for repairs to the roof. On my own, I contacted four roofing contractors and got their bids. Two of them were modest, the third was a lot higher, and the fourth was astronomical. My opponent hadn't done any such homework. I presented him with the two low bids, and after some talking we "compromised" on a figure half-way between those two bids. He walked away quite happy with his "win-win" deal.

So what's a corporate lawyer in a three-piece suit doing tromping all over a grimy roof in an industrial district? Doing his homework and saving his client lots of money, that's what.

The Initial Offer

Preliminary Maneuvering

Whenever possible, try to get your opponent to make the initial offer:

- She may surprise you with something more generous than you had been expecting.

- At the very least, her offer will always be within her own perception of the Deal Zone (i.e., on the "sunny side" of her own MAP).

- Beyond that, you just might be able to learn some things about her (especially to the extent that she's not a skillful bargainer).

If Your Opponent Makes the Initial Offer

Your strong bias should be *against* accepting your opponent's initial offer.

Accepting it can make you look too eager. It may prompt her to try to back out and come back with a stiffer proposal.

When in doubt, your default response to her initial offer should be rejection and counteroffer.

If You Have to Make the Initial Offer

Your default position for your initial offer should be just barely more generous to your opponent than your perception of her MAP:

- If she's the Buyer, just a little bit lower than your estimate of her Maximum Acceptable Price (MAP).

- If she's the Seller, just a little bit higher than your estimate of her Minimum Acceptable Price (MAP).

In Response to an Offer from Your Opponent

Whether your opponent makes the initial offer, or a subsequent counteroffer after rejecting one of your offers, the following should be your guidelines (not necessarily in order of sequence or of importance).

Clarify the Offer as Necessary

If your opponent's offer is unclear in any material respect, get that opponent to clarify the point(s) in question.

Clarification is critically important because

- If you decide to reject, you'll know exactly what you've rejected. If the back-and-forth communication gets muddy down the road, you'll be able to spot any proposal you've already rejected, and you'll save yourself the trouble of considering it.

- If you decide to accept, there will be adequate clarity on all material points, and your acceptance can clinch the final deal.

CLARIFY YOUR OPPONENT'S OFFER

If your opponent can not, or will not, clarify the point(s) in question, you either:

- Enunciate clearly and specifically your own "understanding" of these matters, and move forward loud and clear on that basis until/unless your opponent corrects you, or

- Refuse to proceed with further communications until that opponent does clarify said point(s).

> *Warning!*
> *There's never any legitimate reason for your opponent not to clarify all the material points in an offer he submits to you.*

An opponent who delays, or gives excuses, or otherwise shows reluctance, when it comes to clarifying such an offer, is usually looking to create an excuse for backing out of a (supposedly-finalized) deal at a later time, by reason that there was a "misunderstanding" of its agreed-upon terms.

Throw a Theatrical Tantrum

Utilize your well-rehearsed play-acting histrionics described earlier in this book under "Fooling Your Opponent" above.

These will consist of immediate displays of

- shock and surprise, and/or

- hurt feelings, and/or

"THE TANTRUM"

- emotional upset, and/or

- outraged anger, and/or

- financial anguish, and/or

- slapping your forehead, and/or

- rolling your eyes, and/or

- moaning loudly in agony, and/or

- throwing up your arms in dismay.

The precise nature of your demonstration depends on the circumstances and will vary with each individual encounter. Don't overact, but there's nothing to be gained by underacting either.

Decline Any Offer You've Already Rejected

Maintaining your credibility is vitally important, both in dealing with your current opponent and in dealing with others in your community with whom you may be bargaining in the future.

Therefore you never even *consider* accepting an offer that you had previously rejected.

Some offers can be a little fuzzy on this. You may consider a new offer that's *close* to an offer you had rejected before, but *only* if there is some publicly visible difference between this new offer and the one you had previously rejected. If that daylight isn't there, you decline the offer.

Beware of "Deposit" Offers

Some offers, whether initiated by the Seller or initiated by the Buyer, may encompass some form of up-front partial payment as part of the package. This may be labeled "earnest money," "down payment," "option payment," or some other terminology.

Every set of participants, and every jurisdiction, has its own preconceived traditions, expectations, and laws governing such arrangements. There is no one universally accepted set of definitions and rules that govern them all. Therefore, you have to manage every such transaction individually, and very, very carefully. Some of the salient issues are:

- If the Buyer pays the full-purchase price by the due date, does the deposit get credited to that purchase price? Or is that deposit just a separate payment for the Seller's agreeing to hold the Commodity off the market until the due date?

- If the Buyer doesn't come up with the full-purchase price by the due date, does the Buyer forfeit the entire deposit? Some of it? Is there a sliding scale? Does the Buyer's reason for cancellation make any kind of a difference?

- If the Buyer doesn't come up with the full-purchase price by the due date, is the Buyer still liable for that full-purchase price? Or does the forfeiture of the deposit relieve the Buyer of any obligation to pay the full-purchase price?

- Is the Seller permitted to sell to somebody else prior to the due date? If so, what are the penalties on the Seller? Refund all of the entire deposit? Some of it?

- To whom is the earnest money paid? The Seller? Or a third-party trustee or escrow holder? What are the obligations of any such third party?

> *Warning!*
> *Here's where you definitely need to bring in your lawyer. Don't rely on your opponent's assurances. Get the entire matter clarified, and put it in writing. If your opponent won't put this in writing, walk away from the deal.*

Avoid Partial Agreements

Your focus must always remain on price.

> *Warning!*
> *Many a sly opponent will attempt to introduce one or more additional matters for discussion. Such an opponent may focus attention on one such point and then, having "reached an agreement" on that topic, move on to the remaining subjects. Then if discussions get difficult later on, that opponent can use this "agreement" to try to block you from revisiting it as part of the overall package.*

Do not fall for this trick. Your posture should be that *there's never any final agreement on any one component until there's a final agreement on the entire package.*

Responding to a "Take-It-or-Leave-It" Offer

In a situation that clearly calls for bargaining (i.e., a "Bargained Price" rather than a "Set Price"), some opponents will open with a take-it-or-leave-it figure and refuse to budge from that number.

A player with such an attitude is inevitably an unsophisticated novice who isn't familiar with the expectations and customs of the bargaining process. (Experienced bargainers usually refuse to deal at all, regardless of the consequences, with someone who won't engage in the time-honored give-and-take of reciprocating concessions.)

If such a player presents you with such a demand and absolutely refuses to budge, you must first examine the figure carefully and determine how close to (or far from) acceptability that number may be for you. Then confront your options:

- If you reject, you lose the deal.

- If you accept, you may get the benefits of this particular deal, but consider carefully the implications of such acceptance. What will this do to your reputation within the bargaining community, which is (inevitably) watching this transaction carefully? Will the word go forth that you're a pushover for such tactics in future deals? (And keep in mind always that there *will* be future deals; you can count on that.)

The guideline here is that *you don't deal on such a basis unless you're really desperate*.

Walking Out (Defensively)

Your default line is "I'll give your offer some thought, and I'll get back to you."

You then discontinue the talks and physically depart the premises.

The Defensive Walkout is most useful when your motivation is to stop and get your bearings.

Walking Out (Offensively)

Your default line is "No, I'm afraid your offer just won't work at all. If you'll excuse me, I have another appointment to go to right now. Don't call me, I'll call you."

You then discontinue the talks and physically depart the premises, without leaving any counteroffer on the table for that opponent.

The Offensive Walkout leaves your opponent fearful that you're on the verge of terminating the bargaining discussions, potentially leaving that opponent high and dry without any deal at all. It can be quite useful when your motivation is to soften up your opponent as a prerequisite to extracting further concessions.

If You Decide to Reject and Counteroffer

Select Your Counteroffer Point

This must be a single-point-dollar figure.

To arrive at your counteroffer, examine carefully your (continually evolving) estimates of

- your opponent's MAP,

- your opponent's ability to take a risk, and

- your opponent's ability to take his time.

A lot may have happened since you extended your preceding offer or counteroffer. Therefore, your counteroffer has to be tailor-made every time you make a new counteroffer.

Reject Properly

Make your rejection convincing in principle. Having once rejected this offer, you'll never accept this specific proposal if it's ever resubmitted, so don't give your opponent any leeway to think otherwise.

Do whatever's appropriate to drive home this message.

If and as appropriate, throw a "Theatrical Tantrum" (as described earlier).

Move Swiftly and Decisively to Your Counteroffer

If you delay, your opponent may think you're not serious about the move.

Counteroffer Properly

If you're retreating from a previous position, maintain the credibility of that position and justify your retreat from that position. (See the discussion in "Making a Concession" above.)

Make your counteroffer clear in all material respects:

- So that if your opponent accepts, there's adequate clarity on all material points, and the acceptance clinches the deal.

- So that if your opponent rejects, you know exactly what's been rejected, and you can fashion future offers to avoid what has already been rejected.

Support your counteroffer with a convincing statement (buttressed by any other evidence you can think of) as to why this offer is just *barely* acceptable to you. (See the discussion on "Fooling Your Opponent" above.)

Don't Try to "Bluff" with Your Counteroffer

> *Warning!*
> *Your counteroffering posture is not part of your ongoing program of deception. It is never a "bluff". Don't confuse Bargaining with Poker.*

Remember:

- Poker is a winner-take-all endeavor where you win big if you intimidate your opponent and cause him to drop out of the game.

- Bargaining is a shared-pot endeavor where you lose big if you intimidate your opponent and cause him to drop out of the game.

If You Decide to Accept Your Opponent's Offer

Make sure the offer is clear on all material elements of the deal. Be very careful here. If you feel it's necessary, restate the offer and get your opponent's agreement that you understand it correctly.

> *Warning!*
> *Take your time. Be suspicious of opponents who are trying to rush you. They could be trying to keep you from learning something important.*

> *Warning!*
> *Make sure your opponent's "offer" is truly a legitimate offer, which is designed to become a final deal once you accept it. Beware the slickster who may try to treat your acceptance as just another counteroffer. Don't fall for this trick.*

When you're satisfied that the offer is what you want, state your acceptance

- not too quickly, not too eagerly, but

- clearly, and

- emphatically enough to clinch the deal.

Approaching the Finish Line

> *Warning!*
> *Beware the time-interval after you reach an agree-ment in principle but before you formally ink (or other-wise close) the deal.*

Many a slickster will try to take advantage of your exhila-rated exhaustion, your inevitable desire to go home and cel-ebrate, by slipping something new into the deal when your guard is down. Examples are:

- Sneaking undiscussed provisions into the fine print of a written contract in the hope that you won't notice them, and/or

- Characterizing a "minor" new item as a "custom-ary detail" of *any* closing of this nature (hoping an inexperienced bargainer will be too embarrassed to admit not having encountered such an item before), and/or

- Brazenly asking for a little extra "nibble" at the tail end.

To counter such stunts,

- Be sure you've flushed every component of your opponent's offer out onto the table, clearly, unequivocally, and undeniably, before you accept that offer;

- Pre-read every word of everything you're expected to sign, and make sure that it conforms to your agreement (Better yet, have your well-paid lawyer do this for you.)

- And (ever so slyly) remember that such a development *may* present you with a *really* good opportunity to turn the tables on your opponent by executing "The Walkout" (whether defensive or offensive).

In the immortal words of Yogi Berra, *"It ain't over 'til it's over."*

Finalizing the Deal

Finalizing the deal consists of entering into a legally binding commitment to do what you have agreed to do.

Your strong bias should be to have this commitment incorporated into a written contract, reviewed and cleared by your lawyers, and signed by yourself and your opponent(s). Putting things into writing has several advantages:

- It forces the parties to think ahead to what types of eventualities might occur in this sort of a deal and to discuss and resolve them beforehand while there's ample room for trade-off compromises, rather than waiting for problems to develop downstream where they can seriously disrupt ongoing operations.

- It gives the parties a visible memorial of what they agreed to, which they can use for guidance down the road.

- It avoids the need to rely on fallible human memory for guidance. ("Gee, I don't remember saying that" is an all-too-familiar refrain when you don't have it in writing.)

- Unlike an oral agreement, a written document is legally enforceable.

Warning!
Beware the opponent who balks at entering into a written contract, who insists that a handshake agreement is fine because "my word is my bond", who suggests that wanting a written deal implies that "you don't trust me". The simple fact is that putting the deal into writing is quick and easy. Any opponent who's serious about the matter has no legitimate reason to resist doing so.

Warning!
Get your document printed up and signed without delay, before other matters arise that could make your opponent want to go back and revisit things.

THE PRIZE

And the All-Important Afterglow

You may want to do business with this opponent again in the future. And you'd like this individual to leave with a positive message to spread around the community about this transaction and about you.

At this time it's especially important to remember to control your mouth and your emotions. Don't publicize your win; don't boast; don't celebrate; don't gloat.

Keep your opponent feeling "warm and fuzzy" about the deal he's just concluded. Emphasize to him how he got a really good deal out of the transaction. Don't let him leave the scene with doubts, afterthoughts, or resentments. Stroke his ego by complimenting him on what a skillful bargainer he is.

You'll be sowing the seeds for future success.

Here's wishing you good hunting!

"THE FAREWELL"